{{code creator

CODING ACTIVITIES FOR
BUILDING
WEBSITES
WITH HTML

Published in 2022 by The Rosen Publishing Group, Inc.
29 East 21st Street, New York, NY 10010

Copyright © 2022 by The Rosen Publishing Group, Inc.

First Edition

Library of Congress Cataloging-in-Publication Data

Names: Furgang, Adam, author.
Title: Coding activities for building websites with HTML / Adam Furgang.
Description: First edition. | New York, NY : The Rosen
Publishing Group, Inc., 2022. | Series: Code creator | Includes
bibliographical references and index. | Audience: Grades 7–12.
Identifiers: LCCN 2019014622| ISBN 9781725341142
(library bound) | ISBN 9781725341135 (pbk.)
Subjects: LCSH: HTML (Document markup language)—Juvenile
literature. | Web sites—Design—Juvenile literature.
Classification: LCC QA76.76.H94 F875 2022 | DDC 006.7/4—dc23
LC record available at https://lccn.loc.gov/2019014622

Manufactured in the United States of America

Some of the images in this book illustrate individuals who are models. The depictions do not imply actual situations or events.

CPSIA Compliance Information: Batch #CSRYA22. For further information contact Rosen Publishing, New York, New York at 1-800-237-9932.

Find us on

Contents

Introduction

Creating a website with HTML may seem commonplace today, but the truth is that the technology required to create and share a website—or even go online and browse the internet—has not been around for a very long time. The invention of the internet, which allows different types of computers to network so they can communicate with one another, was a feat accomplished by many people over the course of many decades. The process that led to the World Wide Web and the internet was not a direct or always-obvious path, but it was an important one.

The first computers invented were mechanical, not electronic. These mechanical computers were devices created to help people accomplish calculating tasks more quickly. In 1890, an inventor named Herman Hollerith created a machine to help calculate the results from the United States census. At the time, calculating the census was a task that took years to finish—obviously not an efficient use of the government's time. Hollerith's new machine used a punch card system and completed the complex task in only a few months. His invention also saved the government a substantial amount of money—and foreshadowed the future importance of computing devices. In 1896, Hollerith founded the Tabulating Machine Company. Eventually, this became the International Business Machines Corporation, which is today known as the computer company IBM.

In 1939, a British mathematician named Alan Turing was instrumental in another important milestone in the history of computers. During World War II, Turing was working with the British government as a code breaker to help decrypt Nazi transmissions that were sent in encrypted code. A German machine—called Enigma because it was used to create nearly unbreakable encryptions—created the codes used to hide messages. At the time, the codes created by the Enigma machine were ironclad; no code breakers had been able to develop a consistent method through which they could decrypt these messages and gain valuable intelligence about Germany's plans. Turing, working alongside other code breakers in a group called Ultra, created an electromechanical machine called the Bombe, which was able to decrypt the secret German Enigma codes and greatly aid British and American war efforts. This machine—

During World War II British computer scientist Alan Turing helped to create the Bombe, a device that was able to decipher German Enigma encrypted code signals.

far more advanced than Hollerith's earlier device—was massive, containing 10 miles (16 kilometers) of tightly wound wire.

In 1958, Jack Kilby and Robert Noyce separately invented the integrated circuit, which was also known as the microchip. This invention eliminated the need for large vacuum tubes and larger circuits, and allowed computers to become significantly smaller while maintaining their computing power. The handheld computer devices that are common today would not have been possible were it not for the invention of the microchip.

Another big step toward bringing computers into homes came when friends Steve Jobs and Steve Wozniak famously started Apple Computers in Jobs's parents' garage in Los Altos, California. They formed their company on April 1, 1976. Their first microcomputer kit was called the Apple I. The consumer-grade Apple II was released in 1977 and quickly became the most successful personal computer at the time. In 1984, Apple announced the Macintosh, one of the first home computers with a graphical user interface, or GUI. After the far-reaching success of some of its earliest products, Apple became a public company on September 7, 1984. The Macintosh Plus was released in 1986, by which time Apple had become a symbol for innovation and cutting-edge technology across the globe. In the decades that followed the company's early success, home computers became more affordable, more powerful, and—of course—very popular.

While computer hardware was becoming more advanced and moving from professional to personal use,

Steve Jobs (left) and Steve Wozniak co-founded Apple Computers in 1976. Apple eventually became a leading manufacturer of personal computers and mobile devices.

networking was still in its early days. Before the rise of the internet as it is known today, there was a computer network called the ARPANET (Advanced Research Projects Agency Network). The network began as a government experiment to link computers together over telephone lines so they could share information with one another. The US military also wanted a network with no centralized core or headquarters that could be eliminated by an enemy attack.

In 1989, computer scientist Tim Berners-Lee—now a legendary figure—invented the World Wide Web while working at the European Organization for Nuclear Research (CERN). The World Wide Web is an information-retrieval system that allows storing, sharing, and retrieving computer information. Berners-Lee also devised a way of linking information; this method was called hypertext, or, more common today, hyperlinks. In addition to this, he developed a computer language called HTML, or hypertext markup language, for formatting graphics, information, and text shared on display screens between computers. After Berners-Lee and others set the standards for the internet, more and more home computers were manufactured to connect

Tim Berners-Lee is one inventor of the World Wide Web. He is still involved with his creation and is shown here at the Web Summit 2018 in Lisbon, Portugal.

and communicate with one another using the methods he devised.

HTML is one of the most successful and enduring computer languages of all time; it is still widely used in web design decades after its creation. It will be the basis for these activities, as well. Learning a computer language like HTML is challenging, but it is also exciting. The following activities are designed to help you grasp how the HTML computer language is responsible for the visual organization of text, fonts, colors, images, links, and other elements that are shared through the internet. After learning more about what goes on behind the scenes of a web page, it will be possible—and relatively easy—to make a hobby or a career of web design.

Activity 1

Site Map Journey to a Website

Though it may be tempting to jump right into hardcore HTML coding, it will be more beneficial to start slow. For a little more background on the language: HTML is computer code language that instructs the structure and organization of text, links, and graphics on web browsers. HTML is interpreted by web browsers and is displayed as web pages on those browsers. Websites are made up from multiple web pages. The latest version of HTML is HTML5, which became an official standard endorsed by the W3C (World Wide Web Consortium) on October 28, 2014.

Most of these activities will require access to a desktop or laptop computer; a secure web browser, such as Google Chrome or Apple Safari; and the NotePad application on a Windows computer or the TextEdit application on an Apple computer, either of which can be used to write the code.

This activity, however, will not require the use of a computer—just gather up some paper, pencils, and drawing implements to get started. Before beginning to code with HTML, it is helpful to think about what the web page or website should be about and what it will be called. While the internet has many large and complex websites, such as YouTube and Facebook, most personal websites created by amateur coders are much simpler and smaller in scale.

Some websites showcase photos or art and can be used as online portfolios to share personal artwork or photography. Many professional and amateur artists, designers, and photographers create their own websites to showcase high-resolution images of their work—or pay someone else to do so. Other websites are created in a blog format; blogs generally concentrate on a particular topic of interest and are updated regularly with news and information. Though less popular in an age of social media giants like Twitter and Facebook, blogs are still going strong in certain interest groups.

Brainstorm a list of what your interests are and what you want to showcase or say online, as well who you think might be interested in your website. Having an audience in mind will also help you to narrow down what content you will create for your website.

After thinking up a topic to focus on, the next step is to decide how the pages in the website will be connected—or linked—to one another. Creating a model of how the pages of a website will be linked is called a site map.

When users visit a website, they arrive at the home page—this is the main hub of the entire website. This means it also serves as the navigation page, so anyone visiting can easily navigate to other pages on the website. Site maps generally start with a home page and branch out to the other most important pages from there. Think about your website's home page, what will be listed on it, and the other pages it will navigate to. Use the drawing supplies and paper to create a site map model. Start with a home page and have the other pages branch off from it. These branches will represent the links.

When designing a site map, use boxes or rectangles to represent the different pages and write the name of the page in the rectangle. If there are colored pencils or markers available, it may also be useful to color-code the different pages. For example:

- Home page (could be white)
- About Page (could be blue)
- Blog Page (could be green)
- Photos (could be orange)
- Events (could be red)

Below are several examples of a basic site map.

This site map is about as basic as possible—notice how the home page links to just three other pages.

This site map example is a little more complex; from the home page, users can navigate to several other pages that also have branching options.

Color-coding a site map can make it easier to tell what kind of content each page will feature.

These examples show how a personal or professional website may be laid out. However, blog-based sites are a little different. Because there is not a lot of content outside the daily, weekly, or monthly entries, a blog site map may not have as many separate branches coming from the home page. Instead, the links to other pages in a blog may look something like this:

A blog's site map may look a little different from more traditional websites, but it still has a similar function.

Activity 2

The ABCs of HTML

Pages in books, newspapers, and comics are all organized in a certain way. This method of organization is set by the publisher and printer. A web browser, on the other hand, uses HTML code as the instructions to organize the text, picture files, and graphics into structured web pages. Using HTML, programmers can format their web pages to look exactly the way they want. In this activity, HTML will be used to create some basic text elements that will be displayed on a web browser.

HTML stands for Hypertext Markup Language—that is quite a mouthful. Put more simply, HTML is a language for structuring web pages using text. Compared to some other programming languages, HTML is actually fairly easy to use.

The simplest component in HTML is a tag. All tags come between < > (bracket) characters. Anything located within the opening and closing brackets is used to indicate what the tag does. One standard HTML tag is the <p> tag, used to signify the start of a paragraph.

Most tags in HTML come in pairs, with an opening tag and a closing tag. A closing tag resembles an opening tag—except that it also has a / (slash) character. The closing tag for a paragraph, for example, is </p>. So, any text that comes between the opening <p> and the closing </p> tags will be set apart as a separate paragraph when displayed on a web page. This entire construction is called an element: an opening tag, content, and a closing tag.

In an example paragraph element, any text that comes after the opening <p> tag will be displayed on a browser as text. The closing </p> signifies that the text has ended. Here is an example of a complete paragraph element with content between the opening and closing tags:

<p>This text will be displayed on a web browser</p>

Elements can also contain attributes that provide extra information about their contents. Attributes appear in the opening tag and have two parts: a name and a value. Here is an example of an element with an attribute that will make the text appear green on a web browser:

<p style="color:green">This text will be green on a web browser </p>

In this example, the word "style" is the attribute name and "color:green" is the attribute value.

Empty elements with no end tag are used to give instructions. For example, the tag <br> can be used to insert a line break between blocks of text, or a space between graphics. Empty elements do not need an end tag.

The opening and closing <html> tags enclose an entire document, indicating that it should be read by the computer as an HTML file. The opening and closing <head> tags enclose the heading of an HTML document. The opening and closing <title> tags are used to list the web page title. The opening and closing <body> tags indicate that the main body of text will appear between them. The opening and closing <h1> tags indicate the heading of a document. Think of the <h1> tag as a headline. There are six heading tags, h1–h6, each of which produces a gradually smaller heading size. As mentioned, the opening and closing <p> tags indicate that a paragraph of text will be displayed.

Another important part of HTML coding is a declaration of the version of HTML used in the file. This is written as <!DOCTYPE html>, which should appear at the top of any HTML file. This tag comes before everything else because it is used to tell the web browser that it should be interpreting the text as HTML code.

To jump right in and make an HTML document, open up the NotePad application on a Windows computer or the TextEdit application on an Apple computer. Though each operating system has a different default application for text editing, they both serve the same function: they will be used to write and format HTML code.

The simple "Hello World" application is often the first program used when someone is learning a new programming language. Traditionally, even expert coders will write a "Hello World" program the first time they start up a new language, just to make sure everything is in good shape.

Name the HTML file "activity2.html" and save it to a new folder on the computer's desktop; that folder should be titled "HTML Activities." This folder will also be used for future activities. Type the following HTML code into the text editor:

```
<!DOCTYPE html>
<html>
<head>
<title>Hello Word! This is the Document Title</title>
</head>
<body>
<h1>Hello Word! This is the Heading</h1>
<p>Hello Word! This is the Content</p>
</body>
</html>
```

To view this file after it has been saved, open a web browser and drag the "activity2.html" file onto the web browser screen. The text written in the document should appear, formatted according to the tags.

Take the time to experiment with tags, elements, and different attributes that can be changed. Try adding more text in between the <p> tags and saving the file to see the results. Add <br> tags between lines of text to create line breaks, which can really change the look and feel of a web page.

Activity 3

Text & Hex

In newspapers and magazines, text is often printed in different sizes, styles, and colors to emphasize the importance of different areas or parts of text of a page. Web pages need these differences, too, so people viewing a page can navigate it with as much ease as printed material.

Luckily, HTML gives users all the tools necessary to adjust sizes, styles, and colors of text on a page. In print and on a computer, different styles of text are called fonts. Web fonts are commonly used fonts that are preinstalled on most computers, so they can be programmed into HTML files. Some common font families are Helvetica, Times New Roman, Arial, and Garamond.

Fonts come in all different styles and shapes. Serif fonts have extra strokes off of the main strokes of letters. Times New Roman and Georgia are both examples of serif fonts. Sans serif fonts are missing the extra strokes that a serif font has. Sans serif fonts are often used for signs, headlines, and other things that need to be communicated simply. To change the font style of paragraph text in HTML, use this tag:

```
<p style="font-family:helvetica">This typeface is Helvetica.</p>
```

Text sizes can emphasize and deemphasize different parts of a page. Text sizes are measured in points. A smaller point number makes the text smaller; a larger point size will make the text larger. In HTML, numbers are used to increase or decrease the font size. To change the font size of text in HTML, use this tag:

<font size="6">This is some size-6 text!</font>

Color can be used in many ways with HTML. The W3C has a set of sixteen standard colors for common HTML use: black, gray, silver, white, yellow, lime, aqua, fuchsia, red, green, blue, purple, maroon, olive, navy, and teal. Additionally, HTML hex code uses a six-digit (hexadecimal) representation of a specific color. The first two digits, "RR," represent a value of red; the next two digits "GG," represent a value of green; and the last two digits, "BB," represent a value of blue. Each hex code is prefaced by a pound sign (#). Some examples of HTML hex codes are: #000000 for black, #FF0000 for red and #FFFF00 for yellow. Common graphics software programs like Adobe Photoshop can be used to pick hex code colors. Lists of hex code colors can also be found online for easy access.

Here is an HTML color element:

<font color="red">This text is now red.</font>

Open up a new text editor file and name it "activity3. html." In this file, copy the following HTML code:

```
<!DOCTYPE html>
<html>
<head>
<title>Setting Font Size and Font Color</title>
</head>
<body text="blue" bgcolor="White">
<font size="4">Setting Font Size and Font Color</font>
<br />
<br>
<font face="Comic sans MS" size="7">Comic sans MS Font Size
   7</font>
<br />
<br>
<table bgcolor="black">
<tr>
<td>
<font color="red">RED text on black background</font>
</td>
</tr>
</table>
<br>
<font color="orange" font face="Times New Roman"
   size="5">Times New Roman</font>
<br>
<font face="Verdana" size="5">Verdana</font>
<br>
<font color="red" font face="Comic sans MS" size="5">Comic
   Sans MS</font>
<br>
<font color="black" font face="Helvetica" size="5">Helvetica</
   font>
<br>
</body>
</html>
```

After typing in all this code, save the document and drag it onto a web browser. The page that appears should feature a lot of different fonts, a lot of different colors, and a lot of different text sizes—all according to the styles entered in the HTML code.

Take some time to change the variables of the various tag elements and attributes. Try changing the font names, the font size, and the pick from the standard list of colors. To really customize the color choices, look up some of the many HTML hex color codes online at https://htmlcolorcodes.com and try using them as well.

Activity 4

The Importance of Graphic Design

Graphic design is the art of communicating a message with visual content such as text, shapes, lines, and images. Both print and web-based pages need to be structured and designed so that ideas and content are easy to navigate and clearly understood by viewers.

A graphic designer is an artist who works by hand or by using a computer to design and communicate images for both physical and online media. A graphic designer could work on logo designs, advertisements, page layouts, box designs, and displays. A graphic designer that designs web pages is commonly called a web designer.

User experience (UX) design is a type of graphic design that focuses on every aspect of the design for an application or product. A UX designer might design a mobile phone application and how it operates, the sounds it uses, and even the branding for promotion.

Don Norman, director of the Design Lab at the University of California, coined the term "user experience."

In an interview with Peter Merholz for Adaptive Path, Norman spoke about UX design: "I invented the term because I thought human interface and usability were too narrow. I wanted to cover all aspects of the person's experience with the system including industrial design graphics, the interface, the physical interaction, and the manual. Since then the term has spread widely."

One component of UX design is user interface design, or UI, which is used to design the interface on an application, program, or web page. A UI designer considers the user's experience and how they will be interacting with the various elements and components on any interactive or clickable design.

When thinking of a web page, the first thing to design is—unsurprisingly—the home page. Accordingly, this activity will be to design a home page for a website. Use pencil and paper, colored pencils, and markers to design a home page by hand.

Although websites can be viewed on many devices today, the standard web page dimensions are 1,024 pixels wide by 768 pixels high, at a resolution of 72 pixels per inch. That translates to roughly 13.5 inches (34.3 centimeters) wide by 10.5 inches (26.7 cm) high— so keep that in mind while designing.

Sketch out a few rough thumbnail designs before deciding on a layout. Think about the design choices, including what fonts should be used, what the background should look like, and where text and graphics will be on the page. Many home pages have a navigation bar at the top or along one side. Visit various websites online to see different web page designs to get ideas for your own page.

After sketching out a strong initial design, follow the steps to create a more detailed home page. Remember to keep the design simple, since all the design elements will need to be able to transfer over to HTML code.

- Draw on paper with pencils, pens, and markers.
- Create a top banner for the name of the website to sit above any navigation bars or buttons.
- Add a navigation bar with the names of the pages from the web page's site map. After being created through HTML code, navigation bars will include text buttons that can be clicked to navigate to other pages on the website.
- Add sections for text, graphics, and images.

Now that the home page has been designed, work on laying out options for the other pages according to the website's site map. Consider adding a footer, which goes at the bottom of the home page and is typically used to list social media links and other important information that can be useful for visitors.

Activity 5

Page Building with Tables, Rows, and Columns

To organize a web page, a grid-like structure needs to be established so that text and graphics get aligned into specific areas. This is similar to how a graphic designer would lay out a magazine or newspaper page. With a web page, HTML tables are used to create a grid that organizes information, text, graphics, photos, and more. This activity will be an introduction on how to begin building a page with a grid framework consisting of tables made up of rows, columns, and borders.

Some web pages use simple tables, while others use more complicated tables. Either way, they serve an important function. Banks and shopping websites that list or display a lot of information would use a lot of tables. Each section of a grid is a table cell. Multiple table cells are made up of rows and columns.

Use the opening <table> and closing </table> tag to create a table element in HTML. Other tags inside the opening and closing <table> tags will define the properties of the table that is being created.

Use the opening <tr> and closing </tr> tags to create table rows. The letters "tr" are short for "table row." The <tr> tags fall within the opening and closing <table> tags. Use the <td> tag wish stand for "table data" to create a new table cell. Here is an example of a single table element:

```
<table>
<tr>
<td>row 1, column 1</td>
<td>row 1, column 2</td>
<td> row 1, column 3</td>
</tr>
</table>
```

Here is a complete HTML example of several rows and columns. Use the following HTML code to create a document—titled "activity5.html"—and test it in a browser.

```
<!DOCTYPE html>
<html>
<head>
<title>Tables</title>
</head>
<body>
<table>
<tr>
<td>row1-column1</td>
<td>row1-column2</td>
<td>row1-column3</td>
</tr>
<tr>
<td>row2-column1</td>
<td>row2-column2</td>
<td>row2-column3</td>
</tr>
 <tr>
<td>row3-column1</td>
<td>row3-column2</td>
<td>row3-column3</td>
</tr>
</table>
</body>
</html>
```

Another important table tag is <th>, which stands for table heading. Use the <th>Table Heading</th> element as a heading for a row or a column. It is also important to use an empty table element to represent an empty table cell. Try replacing a <td> element in the code with a <th> tag. By doing this, the <th> tag renders the text in bold on the browser window.

Without instructions, text that falls inside opening <td> and closing </td> tags will just be the width of the text characters that are typed. Because every web page layout will be different, however, some rows and columns need to be broken up and made wider or taller. This allows for more variety on web pages. Use the <td colspan ="2"> tag to widen the row across the width of two columns; the closing tag is still </td> or </th>. Try replacing an opening <td> or <th> with either a <td colspan ="2"> or <th colspan ="2"> tag. Change the number value to see different results. To get the same control over how many cells a column takes up across several rows, use the <td rowspan="2"> tag. Again, change the number value to see different results.

HTML5 uses CSS, which stands for Cascading Style Sheets. Older HTML code did not use CSS. Previous versions of HTML changed main web page attributes with HTML code. CSS makes creating uniform web pages easier by allowing attributes for font styles and table sizes to be defined on several pages, rather than having to be coded in HTML again and again. For example, to adjust the width, spacing, borders, and background color with older HTML code, it would be necessary to use the following <table> tag attributes to make adjustments to the border, background, width, cell padding, and cell spacing:

```
<table border="3" bgcolor="red" width="500"
  cellpadding="20" cellspacing="6">
```

While this older coding can still be used to gain a better understanding of how HTML works, newer websites constructed with HTML5 no longer use them. More information on CSS can be found online at www .w3schools.com/css.

Type the following HTML code and save it as "activity5a.html" to create a web page with several rows and columns and a border. Add more rows or borders in the code to see how changing the variables can look. Use the <td colspan="2"> or the <td rowspan="2"> tags to adjust the layout. Add more text in the elements to see different results. Use the <br> tag throughout large paragraphs to control line breaks.

```
<!DOCTYPE html>
<html>
<head>
<title>HTML Tables</title>
</head>
<body>
<table border="1">
<tr>
<td>Row 1, Column 1</td>
<td>Row 1, Column 2</td>
<td>Row 1, Column 3</td>
</tr>
<tr>
<td>Row 2, Column 1</td>
<td>Row 2, Column 2</td>
<td>Row 2, Column 3</td>
</tr>
```

```
<tr>
<td>Row 3, Column 1</td>
<td>Row 3, Column 2</td>
<td>Row 3, Column 3</td>
</tr>
</table>
</body>
</html>
```

Activity 6

Embedding Images

Images and graphics are an important part of every website—but this was not always the case. When HTML was first introduced, images could not be displayed using the code. As time went on, updates were added out of necessity.

With HTML, it is possible to use different image file formats to add graphics and images to a website. One of the oldest and most common is the JPEG file format. JPEG stands for Joint Photographic Experts Group, the organization that created the file format after being formed in 1986.

A JPEG is an image file that can be compressed to different file sizes. Compression allows a file to become smaller and easier to communicate across computer networks. Compressing image files to a small size was very important with early networks that were simply not capable of handling large files.

Another common image format is the GIF, which stands for graphics interchange format. The internet service provider CompuServe created the GIF format in 1987 so that short animation files could be displayed on the internet. A few other common file formats are TIFF, BMP, and PNG. All of these formats have their strengths and weaknesses, but they are all compatible with HTML.

Use a digital camera or a mobile phone to create four JPEG images—in other words, take four pictures. Make sure all four unique images are the same size. To ensure the images are the same size, it may be necessary to crop them. Many mobile phones and computers have built-in image editors that allow users to crop images to a new proportion. There are more advanced image editing software options, such as Adobe Photoshop, but in general, the editors in most phones and computers will do the trick. Google also has an online image editor for cropping images to a specific size. Internet images are displayed at 72dpi (dots per inch), so be sure that the images' resolution is set to that when using any image editing software.

Once all four images for the web page have been created, they will need to be stored in a specific folder. Create a folder called "Activity6" on the desktop. Inside that folder, create another folder called "Activity6_Images" and place the four images at that location. Now, create a new HTML file named "Activity6.html" and route that file into the "Activity6" folder. This will keep all the files organized and help the HTML document easily access the images.

To allow HTML to access an image, that image will need to be stored somewhere on the internet or on a local device—in this case, the computer. The HTML tag for accessing and inserting an image into a web page is <img>. A common image element would look like this:

```
<img src = "https://internetwebsite.com/imagefiles/movieart
   /image.jpg"/>
```

The "img src" part of the tag stands for image source. The text that falls within the quotes is the link to exactly where the image is being stored. For this activity, the images used will be the ones located in the "Activity6_Images" folder on the desktop. To find out the exact path of each of the four images on your computer—so that the HTML document knows where to retrieve them from—simply drag the images, one at a time, from the "Activity6_Images" folder onto an open screen of a web browser. The image's path will be displayed at the top, in the URL address field.

Here is an example of what a JPEG image path on your computer will look like:

file:///Users/YourUsername/Desktop/Activity6/Activity6 _images/image1red.jpg

Here is an example of what an externally sourced image from the internet would look like:

https://www.mywebsite.com/fiolder/assets/image.jpg

Copy each image's address path and insert them between the quotes of the following image element.

<img src = "[Address path here]"/>

A complete image element that looks like this:

<img src="file:///YourUsername/Desktop/Activity6/Activity6 _images/pic1.jpg"/>

Type up the following HTML code into the "Activity6 .html" file, adding the four separate image address paths into the element:

```
<!DOCTYPE html>
<html>
<head>
<title>Activity6</title>
</head>
<body>
<table border="1">
<tr>
<td>Row 1, Column 1, Image 1
<br>
<img src="[Address path for first image]" />
</td>
<td>Row 1, Column 2, Image 2
<br>
<img src="[Address path for second image]" />
</td>
</tr>
<tr>
<td>Row 2, Column 1, Image 3
<br>
<img src="[Address path for third image]" />
</td>
<td>Row 2, Column 2, Image 4
<br>
<img src="[Address path for fourth image]" />
</td>
</table>
</body>
</html>
```

Once this is complete, opening the HTML file will produce a web page with a two-by-two grid, each square containing one of the linked JPEG images.

Activity 7

Everything but the Kitchen Sink

Building a functional and engaging website requires the use of design, page structure, text formatting, and different types of media. Using concepts introduced in the earlier activities, this activity will be the start of a process to develop a more complete home page that can feature a lot of content.

HTML elements—including tables, headings, paragraphs, and images—are the core building blocks of any good web page. They can be combined, stacked, or nested to create different layouts. For example, a single header tag could include multiple font tags to display a multicolored banner of text:

```
<h1><font color="red">H</font><font color="green">i</font><font color="blue">!</font></h1>
```

It is possible to use HTML to emphasize some text that is important to a website's visitor, while also downplaying other areas of text that could be distracting. Endless combinations will allow for an infinite number of design choices, so anyone can personalize what they create to make unique pages.

When working to turn a paper sketch design into a website, it is best to build a shell—working from the outside in—and to frequently test the HTML code to make sure it works properly. Creating a web page also requires something of an artistic touch. Imagine writing a report or an essay: typically, the beginning is at the top of a page and all the elements of the work proceed straight down. When coding a website with HTML, however, it is helpful to think about it like creating artwork. In a still life painting, for example, the artist would begin by defining the shape and lines of the objects. Once happy with how that looks, they would move inside the lines to add color, shading, and more details. This activity will work in a similar way: starting with the structure of the web page—filling things in with placeholders—and then moving on to ironing out and inserting the details later.

When making changes to code, it is worth frequently checking how the page looks in a browser as it is coded and making adjustments if needed. Remember that the paper sketch design of the web page is just a guide—it is perfectly okay to change aspects of it as the page comes to life on the screen. As the code comes together, consider how someone will interact with the page. Is the most important information up top? Is it easy to find the navigation to other pages? Is the text easy to read?

Open up a new file and name it "activity7.html." This should be saved in the "HTML Activities" folder. Then, use the following code to get the web page design up and running:

```
<!DOCTYPE html>
<html>
<head>
<title>My Website</title>
</head>
<body>
<table border="2" bordercolor="blue" width="500">
<tr>
<td colspan="2"><h1>My Website</h1></td>
<td colspan="3"></td>
<td colspan="2">Logo Goes Here</td>
</tr>
<tr>
<td width="14%">Home</td>
<td width="14%">About</td>
<td width="14%">Blog</td>
<td width="14%">Photos</td>
<td width="14%">Events</td>
<td width="14%"></td>
<td></td>
</tr>
<tr>
<td rowspan="2" colspan="2">
<h2>News</h2>
<p>This is where the news goes</p>
</td>
<td colspan="5">Photos Go Here</td>
</tr>
<tr>
<td colspan="5">Artwork Goes Here</td>
</tr>
</table>
</body>
</html>
```

Open the HTML file to see the results. It should look something like this:

My Website		Logo Goes Here
Home	About	Blog	Photos	Events		
News This is where the news goes	Photos Go Here	
	Artwork Goes Here	

This HTML code will be translated into a graphic image with different fonts, test sizes, and tables, rows, and columns.

Now that the basic layout of the page has been established, try adjusting the styling of the header and text. Give the navigation bar running across the table a different look. Adjust some of the text to appear differently, with different fonts or colors. Try making the table bigger with a different border, or make the logo box a little wider. How would you adjust the table to make these suggestions a reality?

Activity 8

The Missing (Hyper)link

A web page by itself can be interesting, but the links on the page allow the person visiting to interact with the website and navigate elsewhere. Links turn standalone web pages into a multi-page site with easy-to-use navigation. A web page design with smartly placed links will allow multiple pages or even different websites to connect to one another. In this activity, the goal will be to turn the text on a page into interactive links, as well as changing some formatting.

The network of pages navigated by browsers on the internet was named the World Wide Web because of its web-like structure. Hyperlinking between web pages, documents, and files is what creates this web. In fact, if the web were mapped out visually, it would resemble an infinitely complex version of the site map created in the first activity. The Web is made up of a multitude of sites and pages hyperlinked together. The mapping of the Web is generated by these links, which web crawlers— software that automatically reads and catalogs content from websites—use to locate and index content for search engines, such as Google.

A hyperlink is created with an anchor tag: <a>. Any text between the opening <a> and closing </a> creates a complete hyperlink. Links have several attributes, the most important of which is "href," which defines the destination of the link:

```
<a>This link goes nowhere</a>
<a href="elsewhere.html">This link goes to another page</a>
```

Links to pages or files on a website use a relative location. That is, the "href" is relative to the page; links to other websites are absolute, on the other hand, and must include the full website path.

Another common attribute of the anchor tag is its "target," which determines where the link opens. By default, clicked links open in the current browser window or tab, replacing the page currently being viewed. By setting its target to "_blank," a link will open in a new window or tab in the browser. This will allow the orginal page and the new page from the link to be open at the same time, rather than the link replacing the original page. Using this attribute can come in handy to keep people on a website, which makes things more convenient for them.

Links can be formatted similarly to other blocks of text within HTML. Links on a web page can look different depending on how the user interacts with them. A link will typically appear as a different color—commonly, blue—than the rest of the text. A link will also typically change color when a mouse cursor hovers over it. These differences and changes allow a user to know what is a text link and what is not. These different states of a single link can be created by using colors as part of a page's opening <body> tag. It is possible to define the colors for the properties of a link. Using "link," "vlink," and "alink" will change the presentation of unvisited links, visited links, and links at the moment they are clicked across the page, respectively. Modern web browsers allow for more formatting options using CSS, including specifying "hover" formats used when the cursor is placed on the link. Individual links can have their colors overridden using the CSS "color" property.

```
<body link="red" vlink="green" alink="blue">
```

Use the following HTML code to create a document called "activity8.html" that will contain several sample links:

```
<!DOCTYPE html>
<html>
<head>
<title>Activity 8</title>
</head>
<body link="red" vlink="green" alink="blue">
<p><a href="activity5.html">Activity 5</a></p>
<p><a href="activity6.html" target="_blank">Activity 6</a>
   </p>
<p>View the <a href="activity7.html"
   style="color:grey;">Activity 7</a> page</p>
<p><a href="https://html5-editor.net">Absolute link to another
   website</a></p>
<p><a href="folder/page.html">Relative link to a page inside a
   folder</a></p>
</body>
</html>
```

Open the file in a browser and try clicking on the links. Notice how the link colors change based on which links have been previously visited or clicked on. Try changing the colors within the <body> tag to adjust the appearance. Experiment with the "target" attribute. In this form, the link to Activity 7 does not change color, even when clicked; remove the CSS "style" attribute so it will behave like the other links.

Most likely, the last link on the page shows an error when clicked. Look at the link's "href" attribute and see if it is possible to fix the link by placing a "page.html" where the link expects to find one, within a "folder" on the computer. Revisit the site map from the first activity and think about how it might be possible to structure the links to the various pages to make them more convenient.

Activity 9

Hyperlinking Images

Since links are some of the most important parts of modern websites, this activity will build on the hyperlinking skills from earlier by using images—rather than text—to create more engaging interactive links.

When building a website, the main function of links is to connect to different pages as well as additional content. Images on the page often stand out more obviously than text—this is why images are often used instead of text to represent links for the thing a website developer wants most people to focus on. After all, people are more likely to click on an interesting graphical button instead of a boring old link that just says "Subscribe Now."

Another common use for images in links is to communicate a function with a graphic. A link to send an email is made clear when accompanied by an image of an envelope, for example. Likewise, a link attached to a magnifying glass shows a user without words that clicking it will allow the user to search for something. Enclosing both an image and text within an <a> tag will allow the two elements to behave as a single linked item. Graphical symbols make it obvious what is likely to happen when something is clicked, and can often communicate their intent no matter what language a person speaks, making them ideal for navigational buttons.

So far, these activities have demonstrated using links to navigate between web pages. However, links can also point to any file type, including JPEG images, PDF text files, and MPEG videos. If a browser knows how to display a specific file, it will do so. If it cannot display the file, it can be downloaded to the user's computer. Linking to image files can be used to create interactive photo galleries, music playlists, and web-based libraries. When hosted on the internet instead of on a local computer, a linked file can be forced to act as a download, bypassing the browser's attempt to display it. This can be inserted by using the "download" attribute:

```
<a href="my-image.jpg" download>Save my image</a>
```

Open up a new text editor file and name is "activity9. html." Remember the images created in Activity 6? They will be used again in this sample code:

```
<!DOCTYPE html>
<html>
<head>
<title>Activity 9</title>
</head>
<body>
<h1>My Gallery</h1>
<p>Or return to Activity 6:</p>
<p><a href="Activity6.html"><img src="[Address path for first
   image]"></a></p>
<table width="310" border="0" cellspacing="5"
   cellpadding="0">
<tr>
<td width="100" align="center">
<a href="[Address path for second image]"><img src="[Address
   path for second image]" width="100"><br>Image 1</a>
</td>
```

```
<td width="100" align="center">
<a href="[Address path for third image]"><img src="[Address
  path for third image]" width="100"><br>Image 2</a>
</td>
<td width="100" align="center">
<a href="[Address path for fourth image]"><img src="[Address
  path for fourth image]" width="100"><br>Image 3</a>
</td>
</tr>
</table>
</body>
</html>
```

Explore the image gallery and observe how the smaller images are used to link to their full-sized versions. Try changing the full-size images to open in a new window or tab, so the visitor is not navigated away from the rest of the gallery when clicking. Change the image captions to better suit the images, and adjust the links to only include the images—not the caption text.

If the images were hosted online and the website wanted to allow visitors to download them, the following could be added after each caption to create a second link:

```
<a href="[Address path]" download>Download</a>
```

Activity 10

Finding Bugs in the Code

Everyone—from elementary students to polished professionals—makes mistakes when writing. From making simple typos to misunderstanding complex grammatical rules, nothing is ever quite perfect. In printed text, editors go over every word to make sure things are right—because in professionally published texts, clarity and correctness are both extremely important attributes. This attention to detail is also very important when writing computer code.

When mistakes happen in regular writing, the reader can often figure out what the intended message was. Context clues and background knowledge can fill in the gaps that an author unintentionally leaves. In programming, however, things are not always so easy. In HTML, an error can be small and not create a problem. However, sometimes HTML coding mistakes can cause a web page to display improperly, or a link to be broken and not take the user where they should be going. This is because computers cannot fill in the blanks, so to speak—they are machines that can only do exactly as they are instructed. As such, checking for broken or buggy code is a crucial part of the programming process for everyone.

Testing code means viewing the site as a visitor would, checking out the front end instead of just looking at the back end as a creator or developer. To do this continually, it is possible to view code in a browser and run through the different, links, buttons, graphics, and images in real time. Test everything by double-checking to see that all the code works the way it is intended to.

Some typical problems in HTML include unclosed tags, missing brackets, missing or incorrect formatting, bad nesting, and dead links. When a problem is encountered on the web page, make a note and refer back to the HTML code to locate the mistake and figure out how to fix it.

Below is HTML code with an error that may not seem obvious at first. Type the code into a new file called "activity10.html." After viewing the code in a browser, try finding the broken chunk that needs fixing. If you get stuck, refer to the Answer Key.

```
<!DOCTYPE html>
<html>
<head>
<title>Bugs in the Code</title>
</head>
<body text="white" bgcolor="white">
<table bgcolor="black">
<tr>
<td>
<font color="white">Check the HTML code and find the bug to
   reveal the hidden text</font>
</td>
</tr>
</table>
<p>Looking for bugs requires carefully searching through the
   HTML code to see where a mistake is hiding in plain sight.
<br>Here the HTML tag for the text was white and white for the
   background, making it impossible to read this text until the
   code was corrected.</p>
</body>
</html>
```

After figuring out how to find and squash the bug in this code, try using intentionally broken code to create hidden text on a live web page. This can be a great way to create a blog post so no one can see the text while it is still being worked on. After it is finished, the code can then be "corrected" when the text is ready for an audience. Try inserting broken links into some code to see what happens when it is tested. What does the browser display when a link is broken? How can that be fixed?

Career Connections

When Tim Berners-Lee first created HTML in 1990 as a simple text-based language to make computer-to-computer communications easier, no one could have anticipated the unbelievable growth of the internet and computer science. To meet the increasing demands of computer users, HTML has seen many improvements and updates over the years. Originally, images could not be displayed and HTML was only a text-based language. People soon began adding new tags, such as <img>, <background>, <frame>, and <font> to make things more visually interesting. As more and more companies, such as Netscape and Microsoft, created early browsers, HTML continued to gain additional new features.

As the internet grew in the 1990s and 2000s, millions of people—both amateurs and professionals—started to create their own websites. As time went on, websites have replaced the traditional phone books of the past as the go-to location to find business information and countless other topics of interest. Today, having a website is an important asset no matter what the industry or profession. Whether someone is a doctor, lawyer, contractor, writer, store owner, artist, musician, photographer, or blogger, having a website as a portal for people to visit is important. Websites are also useful communication tools in today's career marketplace.

Websites can be essential for businesses, even small ones, and are typically where many people go to find locations, hours, contact information, and even to shop

Creating a website with HTML can help to communicate many ideas to a wide audience around the world. Websites are a useful tool both for business and for entertainment.

online. Ultimately, a website can help communicate to the world about who someone is and what he or she does in a way that was impossible only a short while ago.

Another useful component of being able to create a website is to help promote oneself while looking for a job. Using HTML to create an online résumé is a great way to showcase unique skills and interests to potential employers.

There are also many websites online to help with the creation of personal and professional websites. Many of the web coding skills here can be applied to more advanced software applications that allow for finer customization with HTML.

Computer coding, in general, has become a very important skillset to have—and an inability to code is quickly becoming a detriment in the fast-paced world of technology. Many consider learning to code an incredibly important part of education today and consider it an important second language that young people should learn. The modern world is more and more technologically advanced every day, and being

HTML is a useful tool for creating websites. Learning HTML can lead to a career as a website designer, software developer, or a computer programmer.

comfortable with complex computers is important for both personal and professional life. In addition, coding is a great way to encourage creativity in young learners, who can be exposed to the limitless possibilities of the programming world.

Because the need to learn coding has become so important, many schools are now teaching coding at younger ages. Programs like Scratch, which uses stackable colored blocks on a computer screen to teach coding concepts, have made learning coding concepts easier. This is good news for anyone interested in learning more about computer science, regardless of age. There are countless resources online that make complicated coding concepts much easier to learn and understand. After learning one language—whether it is a starter structure like Scratch or a more robust language like HTML—it is much easier to learn another. Many of the foundations of computer programming can be carried over across languages—something that is, again, good news for anyone just starting out.

Computer code is truly a language in which it pays to be proficient. Computer languages are becoming the most widely used languages around the world, and programming talents are in high demand, with few skilled coders available to fill the millions of open programming positions at companies of all sizes across the globe. At the cutting edge of technological advancement, there are not only a great number of jobs—but most of those positions are also well compensated. According to the Bureau of Labor Statistics (BLS), computer programmers averaged a salary of more than $84,000 in 2018.

Learning to code with HTML in school is becoming common. Access to mobile computers in schools makes learning to create websites with classmates a fun experience.

Additionally, there are many other occupations besides programming that can make use of a background in computer science. Across all jobs related to the computer industry, the BLS predicts that job growth will increase by 13 percent between 2016 and 2026. In almost any industry related to technology or computers, knowledge of HTML will be a big help. Many modern coding platforms are either built on or inspired by the early days of HTML computing, so the syntax and practices of those languages will be easy to pick up. This is useful, because a programmer who can use multiple languages effectively will be worth their weight in gold in the job market.

Learning to expand on the foundations of HTML—or take up learning any computer language—will be that much easier now that you have a basis for how a web page can be constructed. Learning to code with HTML is a strong first step on the way to a greater understanding of how websites work, how to better communicate with the code that makes browsers run, and how to use this knowledge to seize any available career opportunity.

For someone interested in computer science, web development, or just general programming, the next steps to career readiness are to learn more about different languages—which can be done online or through locally available courses—and eventually move on to getting a bachelor's degree. Thousands of colleges and universities offer programs that prepare students for a career in technology, and having a four-year degree is a common requirement in the field. However, a two-year associate's degree or certificate from an accredited institution can also go a long way toward getting one's foot in the competitive and lucrative industry of computer science.

Answer Key

Activity 10 Solution:

```
<body text="white" bgcolor="white">
```

    This line of code should be corrected to appear as follows:

```
<body text="black" bgcolor="white">
```

Glossary

ARPANET An early computer communications network developed in 1969 by the US Department of Defense; a precursor to the internet.

census A government-run data collection practice used to count the population.

CERN A European organization for nuclear research; the CERN acronym comes from its original French name: Conseil Européen pour la Recherche Nucléaire.

code breaker A person who breaks or decodes hidden messages.

computer code A set of instructions used by a computer or software that allows it to run or perform a variety of tasks.

element In HTML, a distinct set of basic components, such as the tags and contents of an HTML document.

encryption The process of converting a message or communication into code that cannot be understood without decryption.

Enigma An electrical rotor machine that was used to encrypt and decrypt secret messages by Germany during World War II.

font A collection of letters or characters with a similar design style.

GUI The graphics interface of a computer screen that allows users to click and drag computer files as virtual objects with a mouse rather than entering code commands.

HTML Hypertext Markup Language; used to create graphic documents on the internet with text, graphics, sound, video, and hyperlinks.

hyperlink An electronic link that connects from one distinctively marked place in a HTML document to another in the same file, or a different document elsewhere on the internet.

JPEG A common format that is used to compress and store images online.

microchip Also known as an integrated circuit, a small batch of electronic circuits and components created on material, commonly silicon.

network An interconnected system of computers that are able to communicate with each other.

pixel A small dot on a screen or monitor that emits light according to the necessary picture output.

software Blanket term for programs and operating system instructions that run computers and applications.

syntax The structure and constructions permitted within a specific computer language.

web browser A computer software program that allows users to search for, access, and display HTML web pages.

web design The practice of conceiving, designing, and creating websites and other online content, commonly using HTML.

World Wide Web A searchable system on the internet that connects documents to one another with hypertext links.

For More Information

Canada Learning Code
129 Spadina Avenue, Unit 501
Toronto, ON M5V2L3
Canada
Website: www.canadalearningcode.ca
Facebook: @canadalearningcode
Instagram and Twitter: @learningcode
Canada Learning Code is an organization dedicated to
    teaching computer coding to all Canadians, focusing
    especially on women, girls, people with disabilities, and
    indigenous peoples.

Code.org
1501 4th Avenue, Suite 900
Seattle, WA 98101
Website: https://code.org
Facebook: @Code.org
Instagram and Twitter: @codeorg
Code.org is a nonprofit organization that provides access
    to computer science learning in schools, including the
    Hour of Code program.

Google
1600 Amphitheatre Parkway
Mountain View, CA 94043
Website: https://google.com
Facebook, Instagram, and Twitter: @Google
A global search engine that allows users to type keywords
    to locate items in a database on the World Wide Web.

HTML.com
27 Mortimer Street
London, W1T 3BL
United Kingdom
Website: https://html.com
As a coding tutorial website that has been around since
the early 2000s, HTML.com's website features dozens
of how-to articles and tips to help anyone using
HTML code.

Kids & Code
320 Catherine Street
Ottawa, ON K1R5T5
Canada
(613) 862-1412
Website: http://www.kidsandcode.org
Facebook and Twitter: @KidsAndCodeOrg
Kids & Code is a Canada-based organization dedicated
to offering classes, workshops, and events for kids
interested in learning to code.

World Wide Web Consortium (W3C)
32 Vassar Street, Room 32-386
Cambridge, MA 02139
Website: https://www.w3.org
Twitter: @W3C
The W3C is an international community where
organizations, staff, and the public work together to
develop online standards

For Further Reading

Boehm, Anne, and Zak Ruvalcaba. *Murach's HTML5 and CSS3*. Fresno, CA: Mike Murach & Associates, 2018.

Duckett, Jon. *HTML and CSS: Design and Build Websites*. Indianapolis, IN: John Wiley & Sons, 2014.

Frain, Ben. *Responsive Web Design with HTML5 and CSS3*. Birmingham, UK: Packt Publishing, 2017.

Golombisky, Kim, and Rebecca Hagen. *White Space Is Not Your Enemy: A Beginner's Guide to Communicating Visually Through Graphic, Web & Multimedia Design*. Boca Raton, FL: Taylor and Francis Group, 2017.

Lupton, Ellen, and Jennifer Cole Phillips. *Graphic Design: The New Basics*. New York, NY: Princeton Architectural Press, 2015.

Mihajlov, Martin. *HTML QuickStart Guide: The Simplified Beginner's Guide To HTML*. Albany, NY: ClydeBank Media, 2016.

Rickaby, Greg. *Creating a Web Site: Design and Build Your First Site!* Hoboken, NJ: John Wiley & Sons, 2017.

Young Rewired State. *Get Coding! Learn HTML, CSS & JavaScript & Build A Website, App & Game*. Somerville, MA: Candlewick Press, 2017.

Bibliography

Bureau of Labor Statistics. "Computer Programmers." April 12, 2019. https://www.bls.gov/ooh/computer-and -information-technology/computer-programmers.htm.

Isaacson, Walter. *The Innovators: How a Group of Hackers, Geniuses, and Geeks Created the Digital Revolution.* New York, NY: Simon & Schuster, 2015.

Karch, Marziah. "7 Free Programming Languages to Teach Kids How to Code." Lifewire, December 16, 2018. https://www.lifewire.com/kids-programming-languages -4125938.

Kernighan, Brian W., and Dennis Ritchie. *The C Programing Language: Second Edition.* Saddle River, NJ: Prentice Hall, 1988.

Merholz, Peter. "Peter in Coversation with Don Normal about UX & Innovation." Adaptive Path, December 13, 2007. https://adaptivepath.org/ideas/e000862.

Restuccia, Dan. "Five Careers where Coding Skills Will Help You Get Ahead." Burning Glass Technologies. July 18, 2016. https://www.burning-glass.com/blog/five-careers -where-coding-skills-will-help-you-get-ahead.

Trikha, Ritika. "The History of 'Hello, World.'" HackerRank, April 21, 2015. https://blog.hackerrank.com/the-history -of-hello-world.

Veen, Jeffrey. "A Brief History of HTML." *Wired*, April 28, 1997. https://www.wired.com/1997/04/a-brief-history -of-html.

Index

About the Author

Adam Furgang was first introduced to computers in the 1980s when he played the video games *Load Runner* and *Castle Wolfenstein* on his friend's Apple IIe home computer. Before becoming a writer, Adam worked as a web designer in the late 1990s at one of the very first social networks, TheGlobe.com. He has continued to work on computers and runs several of his own websites including a gaming blog, wizardsneverwearamor.com. He lives with his wife and two sons in upstate New York.

Photo Credits

Cover © iStockphoto.com/oatawa; cover, p. 1 © (code) iStockphoto.com/scanrail; p. 5 Album/Alamy Stock Photo; p. 7 Tom Munnecke/Hulton Archive/Getty Images; p. 8 NurPhoto/Getty Images; pp. 12 (both), 13, 37 Adam Furgang; p. 49 Ariel Skelley/DigitalVision/Getty Images; p. 50 AlexSava/E+/Getty Images; p. 52 vgajic/ E+/Getty Images; interior pages border design © iStockphoto.com/Akrain.

Design: Matt Cauli; Editor: Siyavush Saidian; Photo researcher: Sherri Jackson